An American Journey

An American Journey
Images of Railroading During the Depression

Mark S. Vandercook

www.HotBoxPress.com

Hot Box Press, www.HotBoxPress.com/ P.O. Box 161078, Mobile, AL 36616
Design and layout by Mark S. Vandercook

Edited by Joseph P. Gaston

Library of Congress Cataloging-in-Publication Data

Vandercook, Mark S., 1969–

    An American Journey: images of railroading during the Depression/ Mark S. Vandercook

    Includes bibliographical references.

    ISBN 0–970–35444–4

    1. Railroads–United States–History.

    2. Railroads–Social aspects.

    3 United States–Farm Security Administration I. Title

TF23V36 2000   00-107569

385' .0973   CIP

Printed in Canada

Printed on acid-free paper   05 04 03 02 01 C 5 4 3 2 1

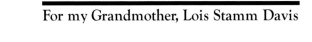

For my Grandmother, Lois Stamm Davis

CONTENTS

PREFACE : ix

INTRODUCTION : 1

PHOTOGRAPHERS : 5

1935 : 13

1936 : 19

1937 : 27

1938 : 45

1939 : 73

1940 : 135

1941 : 155

APPENDIX : 159

SELECTED BIBLIOGRAPHY : 165

PREFACE

It should be noted at the outset that this book is a collective work of several photographers, namely: Jack Delano, Walker Evans, Dorothea Lange, Russell Lee, Carl Mydans, Arthur Rothstein, Ben Shahn, John Vachon, and Marion Post Wolcott. As the author, I have simply collected their work into this volume and, hopefully, added some context.

Out of respect to the photographers, their work has not been cropped. It appears here exactly as originally composed. You will see both rectangle and square photographs, which correspond to the original negative shape and type of camera used. The captions were written by the photographers for the Farm Security Administration (FSA), and in some cases these captions were edited by the FSA. The same caption may apply to more than one photograph. No effort has been made to research the accuracy of the captions. Where, however, a caption is known by the author to be inaccurate, a note below the caption has been included.

Being held by a government institution is hardly the ideal environment for delicate negatives. Many prints were severely scratched, and nearly all were replete with minor scratches and dust marks. Considerable time and effort has been expended in cleaning up the photographs. It has been my intent to make the photographs printed in this book look as pristine as the very first print from the original negative might have looked.

Interurbans and street cars have been included in the mix. A very few railroad purists may scoff at the intrusion, but I believe them to be a close enough derivative to warrant their inclusion. I think these photographs, in particular, help to illustrate the discrepancy between a more affluent middle-class urban population, and the displaced rural poor.

Included in the Appendix is a cross reference with each photograph's Library of Congress reproduction number. Those wishing to order prints of any photograph may contact the Library of Congress Photo Duplication Service. The photographs here do not represent all of the FSA's railroad photographs. There were many excellent photographs taken during the war years (see: James E. Valle, *The Iron Horse at War*, also Ball and Whitaker, *Decade Of The Trains: The 1940s*). There were also many photographs unavailable at the time of printing.

As with any project of this nature, an author must ask for, and rely on, the help of others for various aspects of the work. So, I would like to extend a most heartfelt thanks to one of the hardest working individuals (and one of the best friends) I have ever known, Joe Gaston. His work with the preparation and editing of the manuscript (and everything else) is greatly appreciated. Thanks are also in order for Andrea West for editing of the manuscript. The work of Deborah Evans and the staff at the Library of Congress Photo Duplication Service can be readily seen on nearly every page of this book. Thanks to Wilma Joe and the crew at the Mobile Public Library Inter-Library Loan Department, who never fail to greet me with a smile as I hand them more work to do–Thank you!

INTRODUCTION

As long as I can remember, I have had a fascination with trains. For those not of a similar disposition it may seem odd, this connection with a seemingly inanimate object. But therein lies the key, for those blessed with the knowledge, trains are not inanimate. Steam engines, in particular, are living, breathing, snorting, industrial-age dragons, and it was no accident they were nicknamed "iron horses" in the 1800s. To then expand the subject from trains to railroads is to add a whole new dimension to the fascination. For locomotives and their cars don't make a railroad, people do. Along those same lines, what would a railroad be without the patrons it serves?

As we enter into this new century, it's easy to take the railroads for granted. It's even easier to overlook them completely, but this wasn't always so. During the period in question, the Depression years of the 1930s and the prewar 1940s, railroads were entrenched in every facet of American life. Physically, the railroads were an imposing feature of the terrain, covering nearly 250,000 miles (the number today is about half that). There were few places of any measure of importance or population in the lower 48 states not located along rail lines. Emotionally and culturally the railroads were a favorite of song, film, stage, and fiction. Both physically and in fantasy they offered an escape from the small town to the big city at the end of the line. Ingrained in every aspect of Depression era life, these steel gossamer threads bound the nation. Our preoccupation with railroads was exemplified by the popularity of both the Lionel and American Flyer toy trains of the period. There were at this time, in fact, more Lionel models run by would-be engineers than the real thing.

The 1930s, at least in America, are most remembered for the Great Depression. The catastrophe of the stock market crash followed by the midwest's "Dust Bowl," brought on by a massive drought, produced a time of suffering unparalleled in American History. When trying to scrape together enough money for food, many parents during this time could not afford luxury items such as Lionel trains for their children. Despite these tragedies the railroads continued to flourish. Whole new castes of Americans arose around the railroads: hobos, boomers, itinerants, bums, tramps, each with its own niche, but with the commonality of bumming a free ride. Up until this time, Americans had long prided themselves on a classless society. Compared to Britain where passenger cars had always had compartments to help separate the classes, American coaches were much more democratic in there utilitarian seating. One can see classism arising in the 1870s with the "immigrant trains" that moved westward carrying human cargo like cattle. During this same time, fancy extra-fare Pullman cars appeared, providing an escape from the common coach, or perhaps, from the common man in the coach.

In the 1930s the freight train had become the underpriveleged's "immigrant train." The problem historically faced by those considered lower class is that they are easily ignored. Some estimates put the number of migrant workers on the rails during the Depression at one and a half million. But the Dust Bowl area of the midwest might just as well have been a foreign country to many Americans. Without the aid of devices such as television, it was difficult to convey the enormity of the human and environmental tragedy of the Dust Bowl. This was the job of the still photographer. By the 1930s, advances in photography allowed the photographer to easily document an event as it happened. The photographers for the Farm Security Administration (FSA) and its predecessor, the Resettlement Administration (RA), took the concept of "documentary photography" to new levels.

The FSA was one of numerous New Deal government programs designed to aid a desperate populace. Nearly all of the various government departments in this field kept extensive photographic records of their work. Although there was much conservative resistance to this type of "propaganda," it was widespread. Defenders of the practice argued that if no one knew of the programs, they could not possibly do any good. The FSA at once took a more liberal approach than its counterparts by allowing its photographers almost free reign to document the cause and effect of the social upheaval unfolding before them. Headed by Roy Stryker, the FSA sought out some of the most talented photographers of the era. Both Dorothea Lange and Arthur Rothstein, whose photographs are liberally excerpted here, would become leaders of the "documentary photography" style which they helped redefine with their FSA photographs. In doing so, The FSA photographers became more than mere documenters. In many cases the FSA photographs (exhibited widely in art houses, in such magazines as *Life* and *Look*, and through many other venues) became the catalysts for social and political change. As part of a new school of realists in the arts, these photographers and their work influenced everything from John Steinbeck, to the casting and look of John Ford's movie version of Steinbeck's *The Grapes Of Wrath*, to the great populist composer, Woody Guthrie. They ultimately led directly to decisions made by the United States Congress. One cannot, then, look at these photographs as merely detached documentation of a time and place.

The photographs contained here are by definition of a narrower focus, however. One will not find Dorothea Lange's internationally famous *Migrant Mother*, or Arthur Rothstein's *Dust Bowl* among the photographs selected. This is, after all, a book about railroads - or is it? Take a look at the lonely railroad tracks fading into the distance on page 129. Compare it with the photographs on pages 22 and 71. Can these all be photographs of the same thing? In the first we see FDR on the platform of a private railroad car. The last is a freight car being dwarfed by a massive grain silo. If viewed separately, the principle subject of each of these photographs would not appear to be the railroad, and, in fact, none of the photographs in this book are officially categorized under "Railroads" by the Library of Congress. This may be because, unlike most people who photograph trains, the FSA shooters usually had an ulterior motive for photographing their subject. They were interested in a larger picture. How did this object, this common carrier, this massive corporation, this struggling short line, this lifetime employee, how did they all interact with the community, or the community with them? What did the train, its condition, cargo, or location symbolize?

While examining these photographs, it may be possible to come to the erroneous conclusion that the railroad is nothing more than happenstance, a seeming accident of time and place. The first photograph, *Striking miners, Scotts run, West Virginia* on page 14, is a good example. For an instant I debated whether or not to include it. As the title suggests, it's a photograph of striking miners. In the background is a hopper car. Imagine, however, the same photograph absent of the PMcK&Y hopper car. From a purely aesthetic point, the photo is a bust. But what of the inherent symbolism of the striking miners in front of a coal car? Further dissecting the photograph, does the idle and empty car have any relevance to the strikers and the success of their cause? The inclusion of the hopper car further emphasizes the fact that this strike in Scotts Run, West Virginia, was not a local, but a national issue. Where and to whom would this coal be destined, and would the end user have any notion of the oppressive working conditions that bore it?

One of my favorite photographs in this collection is *Coal miners child taking home kerosene for lamps. .* , on page 52. The photograph would not have anywhere near the stunning visual impact it does without the train of overflowing coal hoppers snaking through town, encroaching closer and closer to the porches and psyche of the townspeople. How must this child regard the railroad that intrudes so snugly and overwhelmingly around her? Is it considered a lifeblood, or another link in a chain of oppression? Is it a nuisance, or is it ignored much like most suburbanites today see, but fail to see, the omnipresent power and phone lines entangling nearly every quarter of their sky?

Viewed as a group, I hope one can begin to see the enormity of railroading in this country in the 1930s and prewar 1940s. It surely did touch most every American life in some fashion. The way of life depicted in these photographs, what could be called collectively the "railroad culture," has long since vanished. The railroads themselves continue to thrive, but are no longer a part of our national consciousness. They are, for the most part, invisible. We have these photographs, then, to remind us of an extinct culture, or, at the very least, a distinct era never to be forgotten. The railroads themselves have long been a favorite of songwriters because the image of a train can covey so many emotions: the lonesome whistle, the girl who left on the train never to return, the joy of a reunion when a train brings another loved one home, the brave engineer. A train can be a metaphor for just about anything an imaginative lyricist can think of. The images presented here may be only slightly less open to interpretation and imagination than those conceived by a listener of a song. Certainly the visual is set. A caption, usually vague, sometimes with a little more detail, gives just enough information to start the steel wheels of imagination rolling.

PHOTOGRAPHERS

Jack Delano, 1914 - 1997 (1 photograph)

Jack Delano was already an accomplished photographer when he joined the FSA in 1940. Born in Kiev, Ukraine, in 1914, he emigrated to the United States at the age of eight and his family settled in Philadelphia. In the 1930s, while studying at the Pennsylvania Academy of Fine Arts, he was awarded a traveling fellowship to study in Europe. He picked up a camera to record his travels and found his calling. With backing from the Federal Arts Program in 1939, he produced a photographic study of the lives of bootleg coal miners in Pennsylvania. His photographs came to the attention of Roy Stryker and when Arthur Rothstein left to join *Look* in 1940, Delano replaced him at the FSA.

In 1941 he was sent to photograph in Puerto Rico, where he quickly fell in love with the island and its people. He soon made his permanent home there. Delano organized Puerto Rico's first documentary film department and graphics workshop. He later became the director of the Puerto Rican government's radio and television network. Along with photography, Mr. Delano was a prolific composer, cartoonist, graphic designer and children's book author.

Walker Evans, 1903 - 1975 (1 photograph)

Walker Evans is perhaps the most highly revered of all the FSA photographers. His straight forward, detailed depictions of his subjects have been influencing photography since the 1930s. Evans, who was born in St. Louis in 1903, first began to pursue photography in New York in 1928. By 1933 his photographs were being exhibited at the New York Museum of Modern Art.

Evans became part of the FSA team in 1935. During the summer of 1936, he took a leave of absence from the FSA to work on a *Fortune Magazine* piece with James Agee. The two lived with, and documented the lives of, Alabama sharecroppers for two months. When the piece was rejected by *Fortune*, it was published as a book, *Let Us Now Praise Famous Men*, and remains a seminal work. Differences with FSA head, Roy Stryker, led to Evans' resignation. He became a writer and the only staff photographer for *Fortune* in 1945. He stayed with the magazine until 1965 when he became a Professor of Graphic Design at Yale University. Walker Evans has been the recipient of numerous awards and exhibitions.

Dorothea Lange, 1895 - 1965 (8 photographs) ═══════════

Dorothea Lange came to prominence largely through her work with the FSA. She focused on people, and she had a unique gift which allowed her to quickly put strangers at ease, resulting in some of the most striking photographs of the Depression. Her *Migrant Mother* (1936) is one of the most remembered photographs of that time, and one of the most reproduced in history.

Born in Hoboken, New Jersey, Lange contracted polio at an early age. Leaving her with a lifelong limp, she believed her affliction gave her an insight into the suffering of others. It also gave others an insight into Lange, and helped her subjects (many of whom could be described as victims) accept her more readily. Lange studied at Columbia University in 1917 and 1918 under photographer, Clarence White. Later, in 1918, she relocated to San Francisco where she set up her own studio in 1919, taking portraits of the cities wealthy elite. Lange married the painter, Maynard Dixon, in 1920 and remained a portrait photographer until one fateful day in 1932.

The Depression was in full swing by 1932 and Lange could see the homeless lining up for bread not far from her studio. For the first time she ventured outside the studio to take a photograph, *White Angel Bread Line*, which remains today one of her most famous. She then began to venture out more and more. She worked for the California Rural Rehabilitation Administration in 1935 with a U. C. Berkeley economist, Paul Taylor, whom she later married after her marriage to Dixon ended in divorce. Her work with the California Rural Rehabilitation Administration helped convince Washington to set up a similar photographic unit with the FSA.

Lange worked for the FSA from 1935 to 1942. She worked for the War Relocation Agency in 1942, where she documented the internment of Japanese

Dorothea Lange - 1936

Americans. From 1943 to 1945 she worked for the Office of War Information. Poor health kept her off the scene for many years, until 1954-1955, when she worked as a staff photographer for *Life* magazine. In 1958 she returned to the life of freelance photographer which she maintained until her death in 1965.

Dorothea Lange has been honored with countless exhibitions and is considered one of the most influential photographers of her time.

Russell Lee 1903 - 1986 (35 photographs)

Russell was born and reared in Ottawa, Illinois. His father left at an early age, and his mother died when he was ten. He was shuffled between various friends and family until he went to college to study chemical engineering. He took a nine to five job making roofing products and was thoroughly bored with it. He married an amateur painter in 1927, which intensified his yearning for something more in life. In the fall of 1929, one month before the stock market crash, Russell left his job and the Lee's moved to San Francisco. They immersed themselves in the art scene but soon were off to Woodstock, New York. Russell studied painting with his wife but found he preferred the camera as a medium for his art.

It was at Woodstock that Lee heard about the Resettlement Administration. By that time he had developed a social conscience and the job appealed to him. He met Roy Stryker in Washington and shortly thereafter became a member of the team. He spent most of his time near familiar ground, the midwest. He stayed on the road for months on end, eventually growing apart from his wife who was also engrossed in her work. They were divorced and a short time later he married a Texan named Jean Smith. The two quickly became a team. Jean would write the captions, as well as help to set up multiple flash shots and many other duties.

When war broke out, Lee helped to document the internment of Japanese-Americans. He became directly involved in the war effort by accepting a position with the Air Transport Command, which was documenting air strips and the routes taken by planes. Lee was commissioned as a Captain and was in charge of still photography. After the war, he was tapped again by the government to help document mining conditions. Both Russell and Jean were ready for a break in 1947 and settled down in Austin, Texas.

It was in Austin that his old friend, Roy Stryker, no longer with the government, contacted Russell to do industrial photography for Standard Oil. Russell took the job, but not before debating this marring of art and commercialism. Lee's photo-

Russell Lee - 1942

graphs remain a testimonial to the fact that art can triumph in such a setting. During this period Lee worked for many different corporations, only taking those jobs that aroused his curiosity. Industrial photography was always a part time job for Lee, who continued to document the plight of those less fortunate. He frequently worked for little money if the cause was a good one. In 1965 he accepted a teaching position at the University of Texas at Austin which he held until his retirement in 1973.

Carl Mydans 1907 - (1 photograph)

After considering a career as a boat builder and working as a reporter, Carl Mydans became a photographer. He began photographing out of boredom while covering Wall Street for the *American Banker*. He joined the RA/FSA in 1935. He was the first to introduce Roy Stryker to 35 m.m. photography, and proved to him that it was not just a toy for the amateur as many believed. He joined *Life* in 1936 and went to Europe with his wife, *Life* reporter Shelly Smith, when war broke out. They subsequently covered most of the world's hot spots. The pair was captured by the Japanese during the invasion of Manila in 1941. After a prisoner exchange in 1943 they returned home. Mydans went back overseas in 1944 to continue his coverage of the war. After the war, he was the only reporter to be on the scene and capture the devastation in Fukui, Japan, when the city was leveled by an earthquake in 1948. Mydans also covered the Korean War, receiving *U.S. Camera* magazine's Gold Achievement Award for his work.

Arthur Rothstein 1915 - 1985 (43 photographs)

Like Dorothea Lange, Arthur Rothstein came to prominence largely through his photographs with the FSA, which remain some of the best known of his career. Rothstein was born in New York City in 1915. He received his B.A. from Columbia University where he met Roy Stryker. Photography was a hobby for Rothstein when he took an economics course taught by Stryker. A year or two later, when Stryker was assembling photographs for a never completed book, he began asking around the university for a photographer. His search turned up Rothstein. Immediately after graduating, Rothstein was tapped by Stryker to help set up and organize the photography department of the Historical Section of the RA.

By October of 1935, Rothstein was in the field photographing. In May of 1936, in

Arthur Rothstein - 1938

the badlands of South Dakota, he photographed the skull of a steer bleached by the sun and sitting on a dry cracked riverbed. After his initial photographs, he moved the skull a short distance in front of a cactus patch. The resulting uproar came not from his peers and those deploring the manipulation of the realism inherent in the documentary style of photograph. The loudest cries of foul were heard from partisan and regional politicians who had a political stake in understating the severity of the drought then in effect. The rhetoric was so hot that it became, for a short while, an issue in FDR's reelection campaign. Rothstein laid low and the issue eventually wore itself out.

Rothstein remained with the unit for five years until joining *Look* magazine in 1940. He again returned to government work with the outbreak of World War II, when he became a photo editor at the Office of War Information. Later during the war he became a U.S. Army Signal Corps photographer. After the war, Rothstein photographed for the United Nations for a short time before he rejoined *Look*, where he eventually became the magazine's director of photography. Rothstein stayed with the magazine until it closed its doors in 1971. He later became the photography editor for *Parade* magazine.

Rothstein helped found the American Society of Magazine Photographers in 1941. He edited the society's magazine, *Infinity*, from 1971-1972, and taught at Columbia University from 1961-1970. Throughout his career, Rothstein published numerous books, received countless photography awards, and his work has been the focus of exhibitions worldwide.

Ben Shahn 1898 - 1969 (4 photographs)

Ben Shahn was a well known artist when he joined the FSA, but his experience lay in painting and graphic arts. When he joined the Resettlement Administration it was not as a photographer but as a painter and graphic artist. Shahn had become interested in photography while sharing an apartment with Walker Evans, and, on the advise of Evans, he was transferred to Stryker's photographic division. Mr. Shahn's social conscience, combined with his compositional skills, made him a natural for the type of photographs he was to take with the FSA.

A native of Lithuania, Shahn emigrated to the United States in 1906. By the 1930s he had obtained such a reputation that he was chosen by Diego Rivera to be his assistant for a mural project at the new RCA Building in Rockefeller Center. Shahn did little photographic work after his stint with the FSA ended in 1938. He concentrated instead on other forms of art. In 1947 he became the youngest American painter to be honored with a retrospective at the New York Museum of Modern Art. Mr. Shahn continued to produce respected pieces of art throughout the 1950s and 1960s.

John Vachon 1904 - 1975 (33 photographs)

Unlike most of the other photographers hired by Stryker, Vachon had no camera experience before shooting for the FSA. An unemployed graduate student, he was hired as an "assistant messenger." Vachon was soon overseeing the FSA files where he became familiar with the style and composition of the agency's photographers. Vachon suggested to Stryker that he be allowed to take some photographs around Washington DC to fill some gaps in the files. Stryker recognized that Vachon had talent and he was soon sent out on more assignments. Vachon stayed with the FSA until shortly after it was enveloped into the Office of War Information (OWI) in 1943. He joined the armed forces for the duration of the war. Vachon joined his colleague, Arthur Rothstein, at *Look* magazine in 1948 and stayed there until its demise in 1971. Vachon's photographs have been exhibited at the Museum of Modern Art in New York.

Marion Post Wolcott, 1910 - 1990 (12 photographs)

It seems the only thing about Marion Post Wolcott that was not a mystery was the fact that she had an incredible gift for photography, although even this was often overlooked until the general FSA "rediscovery" in the 1970s. She seemed to emerge out of no where, creating for three frenzied years some of the most striking photographs of the century, only to then vanish from site, never again to seriously pursue her art. A portion of the shroud of mystery was lifted in 1992 with the publication of Paul Hendrickson's *Looking For The Light*, a fascinating study of this complex artist.

Born in Montclair, New Jersey, Marion first picked up a camera while abroad in Austria in 1934. She was intrigued by the new concept of "available light" photography. Back in the states, she began to socialize with the soon to be legendary Group Theater in New York. She made photographs of the motley crew of artists, leftists, and communists, selling prints to her subjects for five dollars each. Around 1936 Marion met the photographers Paul Strand and Ralph Steiner and was invited to

John Vachon - 1942

Marion Post Wolcott - 1940

take the stills for their documentary film shooting in Tennessee. That same year she become a staff photographer for the *Philadelphia Evening Bulletin*, an unheard of position for a woman in 1936.

In 1938 Marion joined the FSA. With some misgivings on the part of Roy Stryker, who didn't like to see such a ravishing young woman traveling alone, she set out in an old car to document America. Marion concentrated on the South and kept up such a frenetic pace that by 1941 she was nearly burnt out from the road. This same year she met a widower by the name of Leon Wolcott, and, after a brief romance, the two were married. Shortly afterward, Marion Post Wolcott resigned her position with the FSA to concentrate on raising a family. Although it seems she intended to resume photography again at some point, for many reasons she never did.

1935

Striking miners, Scotts Run, West Virginia

Ben Shahn - October, 1935

Railroad yards at Williamson, West Virginia

Ben Shahn - October, 1935

Williamson, West Virginia. A railroad yard with cars loaded with coal

Ben Shahn - October, 1935

Railroad yards at Williamson, West Virginia.

Ben Shahn - October, 1935

Bridge and houses in Easton, Pennsylvania

Walker Evans - November, 1935

1936

Freight car converted into house in "Little Oklahoma," California

Dorothea Lange - February, 1936

Housing alongside electric railroad. Milwaukee, Wisconsin

Carl Mydans - April, 1936

President Roosevelt speaking from train. Bismarck, North Dakota

Arthur Rothstein - August, 1936

Pittsburgh waterfront. Monongahela and Allegheny Rivers, Pennsylvania

Arthur Rothstein - September, 1936

Scene in railroad yard. Sacramento, California

Dorothea Lange - November, 1936

Railroad car home of Lloyd Sampson, potato farmer near Armstong, Iowa

Russell Lee - December, 1936

1937

Dock scene, Mobile, Alabama

Arthur Rothstein - February, 1937

Unloading bananas on the dock, Mobile, Alabama

Arthur Rothstein - February, 1937

Yardman on mine railroad, Jefferson County, Alabama

Arthur Rothstein - February, 1937

Boxcar home of flood refugees near Cache, Illinois. About fourteen were living in this car

Russell Lee - February, 1937

During the flood, cows and chickens were moved to the highest ground possible. Near Cache, Illinois

Russell Lee - February, 1937

Unloading express from train. Mount Vernon, Indiana

Russell Lee - February, 1937

Toward Los Angeles, California

Dorothea Lange - March, 1937

Lumber camp locomotive. Forest County, Wisconsin. Note special smokestack to catch sparks

Russell Lee - April, 1937

Boy riding Freight. West Texas

Dorothea Lange - May, 1937

Covered railroad bridge. Jeffersonville, Vermont

Arthur Rothstein - September, 1937

Covered bridge. Northfield Falls, Vermont

Arthur Rothstein - September, 1937

Interior of railroad station. Randolph, Vermont

Arthur Rothstein - September, 1937

Railroad station agent. Randolph, Vermont

Arthur Rothstein - September, 1937

Train arriving from Baltimore. Hagerstown, Maryland

Arthur Rothstein - October, 1937

Interior of railroad station, Hagerstown, Maryland

Arthur Rothstein - October, 1937

Water tower on railroad through Jennings, Maryland. The train now runs only once a week
Arthur Rothstein - December, 1937

1938

Railroad station, Cordele, Georgia

John Vachon - May, 1938

Waiting for streetcar after work, Pittsburgh, Pennsylvania

Arthur Rothstein - July, 1938

Train pulling coal through center of town morning and evenings, Osage, West Virginia

Marion Post Wolcott - September, 1938

Train pulling coal through center of town morning and evening, Osage, West Virginia

Marion Post Wolcott - September, 1938

"Sittin' on the tracks." Mining town, Osage, West Virginia

Marion Post Wolcott - September, 1938

Train pulls coal through center of town past miners' homes (company houses) several times morning and evening, Osage, West Virginia

Marion Post Wolcott - September, 1938

Coal miner's child taking home kerosene for lamps. Company houses, coal tipple in background. Pursglove, Scotts Run, West Virginia

Marion Post Wolcott - September, 1938

Woman (probably Hungarian) coming home along railroad tracks in coal mining town, company houses at right, Pursglove, Scotts Run, West Virginia

Marion Post Wolcott - September, 1938

Even the cow goes home along the tracks, the main thoroughfare. Scotts Run, West Virginia

Marion Post Wolcott - September, 1938

Even the cow goes home along the tracks, the main thoroughfare. Scotts Run, West Virginia

Marion Post Wolcott - September, 1938

Coal miner's children playing around tracks. Note live wires. Chaplin, West Virginia

Marion Post Wolcott - September, 1938

Former inter-urban station of "bust" real estate development, north of New Orleans, Louisiana

Russell Lee - September, 1938

Meeting casket at railroad station. Shelbyville, Indiana

John Vachon - October, 1938

Welding on railroad near Port Barre, Louisiana

Russell Lee - October, 1938

Railroad workers, Port Barre, Louisiana

Russell Lee - October, 1938

Railroad weed burner being fueled, Port Barre, Louisiana

Russell Lee - October, 1938

Locomotive taking on water, Port Barre, Louisiana

Russell Lee - October, 1938

Men sitting on signal tower beside railroad track, Morgan City, Louisiana

Russell Lee - October, 1938

Loading sugarcane from farmer's wagon onto railroad car,
near Broussard, Louisiana
Russell Lee - October, 1938

Negroes sitting on foot of the T&P (Texas and Pacific) railroad station, New Roads, Louisiana. Note frequency of train operations

Russell Lee - November, 1938

Union Pacific yards. Omaha, Nebraska

John Vachon - November, 1938

Railroad engineer. Omaha, Nebraska

John Vachon - November, 1938

Lower Douglas Street, Omaha, is one of the hobo centers of the West

John Vachon - November, 1938

Streetcar motorman, Omaha, Nebraska

John Vachon - November, 1938

Grain elevators along railroad tracks. Omaha, Nebraska

John Vachon - November, 1938

Freight car and grain elevators. Omaha, Nebraska

John Vachon - November, 1938

Tops of grain elevators, stacks of lumber, freight cars. Omaha, Nebraska
John Vachon - November, 1938

1939

General store and railroad crossing, Atlanta, Ohio

Arthur Rothstein - January, 1939

Railroad yards along river, St. Louis, Missouri

Arthur Rothstein - January, 1939

Railroad yards along riverfront, St. Louis, Missouri

Arthur Rothstein - January, 1939

Locomotive in railroad yards along river, St. Louis, Missouri

Arthur Rothstein - January, 1939

Locomotive engineer, St. Louis, Missouri

Arthur Rothstein - January, 1939

[both photos] Passenger waiting in railroad station, St. Louis, Missouri

Arthur Rothstein - January, 1939

Railroad tracks. Williamson County, Illinois

Arthur Rothstein - January, 1939

Men squatting on railroad platform, Raymondville, Texas

Russell Lee - February, 1936

Day laborer resting on sign near railroad platform, Raymondville, Texas

Russell Lee - February, 1939

Negroes sitting on railroad crossing signal, Raymondville, Texas

Russell Lee - February, 1939

Railroad gang, Southern Paper Mill construction crew, Lufkin, Texas

Russell Lee - April, 1939

Railroad. Newark, New Jersey

Arthur Rothstein - April, 1939

Domestic help boarding streetcar, Atlanta, Georgia

Marion Post Wolcott - May? 1939

Caboose in railroad yards. Elkins, West Virginia

John Vachon - June, 1939

Railroad yards. Elkins, West Virginia

John Vachon - June, 1939

Railroad yards. Elkins, West Virginia

John Vachon - June, 1939

Engineer and brakeman in railroad yards. Elkins, West Virginia

John Vachon - June, 1939

Railroad yards. Elkins, West Virginia

John Vachon - June, 1939

Yardman polishing light on railroad switch. Elkins, West Virginia

John Vachon - June, 1939

Railroad station. Atlanta, Ohio

Arthur Rothstein - June, 1939

Northern Pacific freight train going over Bozeman Pass. Gallatin County, Montana

Arthur Rothstein - June, 1939

Cattle guard on railroad. Madison County, Montana

Arthur Rothstein - 1939 June - July

Sign at entrance to interurban terminal, Oklahoma City, Oklahoma [left]
Timetable of interurban terminal, Oklahoma City, Oklahoma [right]
Russell Lee - July, 1939

Woman buying ticket at gate. Streetcar terminal, Oklahoma City, Oklahoma [left]
Man reading newspaper while waiting for streetcar. Streetcar station, Oklahoma City, Oklahoma [right]
Russell Lee - July, 1939

Tobacco and magazine stand at streetcar terminal, Oklahoma City, Oklahoma

Russell Lee - July, 1939

Streetcars at terminal, Oklahoma City, Oklahoma

Russell Lee - July, 1939

People getting off and people waiting to get on streetcar. Terminal, Oklahoma City, Oklahoma

Russell Lee - July, 1939

Streetcar motorman in front of station master's shack, streetcar and interurban station, Oklahoma City, Oklahoma

Russell Lee - July, 1939

Activity around station master's shack. Streetcar terminal, Oklahoma City, Oklahoma

Russell Lee - July, 1939

Station master, streetcar terminal, Oklahoma City, Oklahoma

Russell Lee - July, 1939

Dispatcher, streetcar terminal, Oklahoma City, Oklahoma

Russell Lee - July, 1939

Oilers at streetcar terminal, Oklahoma City, Oklahoma

Russell Lee - July, 1939

Workman climbing on top of streetcar to change wheel on trolley. Streetcar terminal, Oklahoma City, Oklahoma

Russell Lee - July, 1939

Railroad station, Fargo, North Dakota

Arthur Rothstein - Summer, 1939

Grain elevator at railroad station, Fairfield, Montana

Arthur Rothstein - Summer, 1939

Streamlined train, La Crosse, Wisconsin

Arthur Rothstein - Summer, 1939

Railroad yards, Minneapolis, Minnesota

John Vachon - September, 1939

Freight cars loaded with coal, Minneapolis, Minnesota

John Vachon - September, 1939

Railroad tracks, Minneapolis, Minnesota

John Vachon - September, 1939

Freight car and flour mill, Minneapolis, Minnesota

John Vachon - September, 1939

Empty freight car, truck, grain elevator, Minneapolis, Minnesota

John Vachon - September, 1939

Man in hobo jungle killing turtle to make soup, Minneapolis, Minnesota

John Vachon - September, 1939

Streetcar, Minneapolis, Minnesota

John Vachon - September, 1939

Streetcars in car yard, Minneapolis, Minnesota

John Vachon - September, 1939

Streetcars in car barn, Minneapolis, Minnesota

John Vachon - September, 1939

Abandoned streetcar, Minneapolis, Minnesota

John Vachon - September, 1939

Freight train and plowed field. Hardin County, Iowa

Arthur Rothstein - September, 1939

Freight car at potato shed. Tulelake, Siskiyou County, California

Dorothea Lange - September, 1939

Railroad yard behind potato shed from which Klamath potatoes are shipped across the country. Tulelake, Siskiyou County, California

Dorothea Lange - October, 1939

Detail of old railroad station. Small farming town, population 108. Irrigon, Oregon

Dorothea Lange - October, 1939

Mexican children carrying water to old railroad station where many Mexican families live during cotton picking season on Knowlton Plantation, Perthshire, Mississippi Delta, Mississippi
Marion Post Wolcott - October? 1939

Cotton bales to be shipped in freight cars, Knowlton Plantation, Perthshire, Mississippi Delta, Mississippi

Marion Post Wolcott - October, 1939

Western Pacific line runs through unclaimed desert of northern Oregon. Ten miles from railroad station at Irrigon. Morrow County, Oregon [Author's note: Union Pacific, not Western Pacific.]

Dorothea Lange - October, 1939

Railroad crossing. Rio Grande County, Colorado

Arthur Rothstein - October, 1939

Loading sheep into freight cars, stockyard, Denver, Colorado

Arthur Rothstein - October, 1939

Railroad track, Chaffee County, Colorado

Arthur Rothstein - October, 1939

Sugar beets are unloaded into railroad cars and taken to the factory.
Adams County, Colorado
Arthur Rothstein - October, 1939

Freight train going upgrade. Eagle County, Colorado

Arthur Rothstein - October, 1939

Refrigerator cars are precooled before being loaded with potatoes, Rio Grande County, Colorado

Arthur Rothstein - October, 1939

Railroad workers eating lunch, Windsor Locks, Connecticut

Russell Lee - October, 1939

Railroad workers eating lunch, Windsor Locks, Connecticut

Russell Lee - October, 1939

1940

Freight train entering Chillicothe, Ohio

Arthur Rothstein - February, 1940

Waiting with mail for train to Reno. Carson City, Nevada

Arthur Rothstein - March, 1940

Loading mail into railroad car. Carson City, Nevada

Arthur Rothstein - March, 1940

Operating switch at railroad station. Carson City, Nevada

Arthur Rothstein - March, 1940

Burlington Railroad tracks. Hitchcock County, Nebraska

Arthur Rothstein - March, 1940

Train crossing the mountains. Eureka County, Nevada

Arthur Rothstein - March, 1940

Snow shed over Churchill County, Nevada

Arthur Rothstein - March, 1940

Snow shed over Union Pacific tracks. Carbon County, Wyoming

Arthur Rothstein - March, 1940

Boy hopping freight train, Dubuque, Iowa

John Vachon - April, 1940

Waiting for the train to Minneapolis, East Dubuque, Illinois

John Vachon - April, 1940

Railroad station, Grundy Center, Iowa

John Vachon - April, 1940

Railroad depot, Connellsville, Pennsylvania

John Vachon - July, 1940

At the freight station in Elizabeth City, North Carolina

Jack Delano - July, 1940

Waiting for streetcar, Chicago, Illinois

John Vachon - July, 1940

Locomotive with snowplow of narrow gauge railroad, Telluride, Colorado

Russell Lee - September, 1940

Filling locomotive with water at railroad station, Montrose, Colorado

Russell Lee - September, 1940

Loading ore concentrate into freight car of narrow gauge railroad, Ouray, Colorado

Russell Lee - September, 1940

Train coming up the valley on a narrow gauge track, Ouray County,
Colorado. Notice the two engines
Russell Lee - September, 1940

1941

Freight cars in yards, Chicago, Illinois

John Vachon - July, 1941

Freight cars in yards, Chicago, Illinois

John Vachon - July, 1941

APPENDIX

Following is a listing of each photograph's Library of Congress reproduction number, cross referenced with the page number the photograph appears on. By contacting the Library of Congress Photo Duplication Service at (202) 707-5640, one may order prints of any of the photographs seen in this book. More information, including current prices, can be found at the Library's web site: www.loc.gov. A majority of the FSA photographs can be viewed and searched at this site.

1935
Page 14 – LC-USF33-006124-M5
Page 15 – LC-USF33-006197-M4
Page 16 – LC-USF33-006197-M1
Page 17 – LC-USF33-006197-M2
Page 18 – LC-USF342-T01-001171-A

1936
Page 20 – LC-USF34-T01-001762-C
Page 21 – LC-USF34-006006-D
Page 22 – LC-USF34-005302-E
Page 23 – LC-USF34-005389-E
Page 24 – LC-USF34-016101-C
Page 25 – LC-USF34-010072-D

1937
Page 28 – LC-USF33-T01-002428-M3
Page 29 – LC-USF33-T01-002424-M1
Page 30 – LC-USF33-T01-002395-M2
Page 31 – LC-USF34-010249-E

Page 32 – LC–USF34–010264–E
Page 33 – LC–USF34–010285–E
Page 34 – LC–USZ6–1470
Page 35 – LC–USF34–010771–E
Page 36 – LC–USF34–016937–E
Page 37 – LC–USF34–025761–C
Page 38 – LC–USF34–025777–C
Page 49 – LC–USF34–025736–D
Page 40 – LC–USF34–025744–D
Page 41 – LC–USF33–T01–002655–M1
Page 42 – LC–USF33–T01–002649–M5
Page 43 – LC–USF34–026067–C

1938
Page 46 – LC–USF33–T01–001148–M1
Page 47 – LC–USF33–002819–M2
Page 48 – LC–USF33–030139–M5
Page 49 – LC–USF33–030251–M2
Page 50 – LC–USF33–030244–M2
Page 51 – LC–USF33–030243–M4
Page 52 – LC–USF331–030180–M2
Page 53 – LC–USF33–030285–M1
Page 54 – LC–USF33–030164–M2
Page 55 – LC–USF33–030153–M3
Page 56 – LC–USF33–030232–M4
Page 57 – LC–USF33–011614–M3
Page 58 – LC–USF33–T01–001206–M5
Page 59 – LC–USF33–011870–M5
Page 60 – LC–USF33–011870–M4
Page 61 – LC–USF33–011870–M2
Page 62 – LC–USF33–011855–M4
Page 63 – LC–USF33–011860–M4
Page 64 – LC–USF33–011867–M4
Page 65 – LC–USF33–011903–M2
Page 66 – LC–USF34–008909–D
Page 67 – LC–USF34–008910–D

Page 68 – LC–USF33–T01–001307–M2
Page 69 – LC–USF33–T01–001286–M5
Page 70 – LC–USF34–008825–D
Page 71 – LC–USF34–T01–008906–D
Page 72 – LC–USF34–008907–D

1939
Page 74 – LC–USF33–T01–002737–M3
Page 75 – LC–USF33–003027–M2
Page 76 – LC–USF33–002992–M4
Page 77 – LC–USF33–002988–M5
Page 78 – LC–USF33–003027–M4
Page 79 – LC–USF33–003030–M2 (left)
Page 79 – LC–USF33–003029–M1 (right)
Page 80 – LC–USF34–026988–D
Page 81 – LC–USF33–012025–M5
Page 82 – LC–USF33–012015–M4
Page 83 – LC–USF33–012033–M2
Page 84 – LC–USF33–012161–M2
Page 85 – LC–USF34–027168–D
Page 86 – LC–USF33–030339–M2
Page 87 – LC–USF33–T01–001405–M5
Page 88 – LC–USF33–T01–001404–M5
Page 89 – LC–USF33–T01–001403–M2
Page 90 – LC–USF33–T01–001403–M4
Page 91 – LC–USF33–T01–001406–M1
Page 92 – LC–USF33–T01–001406–M2
Page 93 – LC–USF34–026404–D
Page 94 – LC–USF34–027252–D
Page 95 – LC–USF34–027223–D
Page 96 – LC–USF33–012342–M2 (left)
Page 96 – LC–USF33–012342–M1 (right)
Page 97 – LC–USF33–012328–M3 (left)
Page 97 – LC–USF33–012324–M3 (right)
Page 98 – LC–USF33–012343–M2
Page 99 – LC–USF33–012343–M4

Page 100 – LC–USF33–012342–M4
Page 101 – LC–USF33–012324–M1
Page 102 – LC–USF33–012343–M3
Page 103 – LC–USF33–012330–M2
Page 104 – LC–USF33–012329–M3
Page 105 – LC–USF33–012325–M1
Page 106 – LC–USF33–012329–M1
Page 107 – LC–USF33–003066–M2
Page 108 – LC–USF33–003107–M2
Page 109 – LC–USF33–003069–M1
Page 110 – LC–USF33–T01–001461–M4
Page 111 – LC–USF33–T01–001461–M1
Page 112 – LC–USF33–T01–001552–M3
Page 113 – LC–USF33–T01–001458–M5
Page 114 – LC–USF33–T01–001456–M4
Page 115 – LC–USF33–T01–001521–M3
Page 116 – LC–USF33–T01–001513–M2
Page 117 – LC–USF33–T01–001459–M3
Page 118 – LC–USF33–T01–001460–M5
Page 119 – LC–USF33–T01–001459–M2
Page 120 – LC–USF34–028080–D
Page 121 – LC–USF34–021026–C
Page 122 – LC–USF34–021022–C
Page 123 – LC–USF34–021130–E
Page 124 – LC–USF33–030539–M4
Page 125 – LC–USF33–030545–M3
Page 126 – LC–USF34–021070–C
Page 127 – LC–USF34–028476–D
Page 128 – LC–USF33–003410–M5
Page 129 – LC–USF33–003388–M3
Page 130 – LC–USF34–028727–D
Page 131 – LC–USF34–028573–D
Page 132 – LC–USF33–003379–M3
Page 133 – LC–USF33–012438–M4
Page 134 – LC–USF33–012438–M2

1940

Page 136 – LC–USF34–029302–D
Page 137 – LC–USF34–029935–D
Page 138 – LC–USF34–029936–D
Page 139 – LC–USF34–029973–D
Page 140 – LC–USF34–029653–D
Page 141 – LC–USF34–029588–D
Page 142 – LC–USF34–029589–D
Page 143 – LC–USF34–029649–D
Page 144 – LC–USF33–T01–001772–M5
Page 145 – LC–USF33–T01–001708–M3
Page 146 – LC–USF33–T01–001784–M1
Page 147 – LC–USF33–016009–M2
Page 148 – LC–USF33–020570–M5
Page 149 – LC–USF33–T01–001909–M5
Page 150 – LC–USF33–012895–M3
Page 151 – LC–USF33–012886–M1
Page 152 – LC–USF33–012897–M1
Page 153 – LC–USF33–012910–M1

1941

Page 156 – LC–USF33–016114–M3
Page 157 – LC–USF33–016114–M2

SELECTED BIBLIOGRAPHY

Ball, Don, Jr. and Rogers E. M. Whitaker. *Decade of the Trains: The 1940s*. Boston: New York Graphic Society, 1977. Features the work of Jack Delano, John Vachon, and Marion Post Wolcott.

Dixon, Penelope. *Photographers of the Farm Security Administration: An Annotated Bibliography, 1930–1980*. New York: Garland Publishing, 1983

Douglas, George, H. *All Aboard! The Railroad In American Life*. New York: Marlow & Company, 1992. Explores how the railroads shaped American life.

Fleischhauer, Carl and Beverly Brannan. *Documenting America, 1935-1943*. Berkeley: University of California Press, 1988. Good general book on the FSA. Lots of photographs and lots of information.

Hendrickson, Paul. *Looking for the Light: The Hidden Life and Art of Marion Post Wolcott*. New York: Knopf/ Random House, 1992. A fascinating study even if you are not familiar with Mrs. Wolcott's work.

Hurley, F. Jack. *Portrait of a Decade: Roy Stryker and the Development of Documentary Photography in the Thirties*. Baton Rouge: Louisiana State University Press, 1972.

———*Russell Lee, Photographer*. Dobbs Ferry, NY: Morgan & Morgan, 1978

Meltzer, Milton. *Dorothea Lange: A Photographers Life*. New York: Farrar, Straus, Giroux, 1978

Ohrn, Karin Becker. *Dorothea Lange and the Documentary Tradition*. Baton Rouge: Louisiana State University Press, 1980

Stilgoe, John, R. *Metropolitan Corridor: Railroads and The American Scene*. New Haven: Yale University Press, 1983. Investigates the social aspects of the railroads up through the 1930s. Highly recommended.

Vale, James, E. *The Iron Horse at War: The United States Governments Photo documentary Project on American Railroading during the Second World War. With 272 Photos by Jack Delano*. Berkeley: Howell-North Books, 1977